GW00775773

VEGETARIAN FOOD FOR MEAT EATERS

(A COMPLETE GUIDE TO USING MEAT REPLACEMENT PRODUCTS. EAT MEAT DISHES THAT ARE VEGETARIAN BUT SUITABLE FOR MEAT-EATERS!)

ROBERT LINDOP

Contents

INTRODUCTION

A few years ago, not long after arriving at a favourite hotel in Zakynthos, Greece, I was sitting in the dining room with my partner, overlooking the swimming pool and an absurdly, stunningly beautiful 180-degree panorama of sea and sand, the sun firing long, dramatic shafts of orange and deep red as it began to dip below the horizon in preparation for another evening of dining, drinking and bingo. I was explaining to the equally absurdly handsome Greek waiter that I was a vegetarian, who also didn't eat fish. He nodded his head and smiled. 'Ah, I am vegetarian, too! I love vegetables. And big salads. Sometimes with a steak.' Having then been a vegetarian for around forty years, this announcement was deliciously amusing, and it gave me the spark of an idea for this book. How *do* you define yourself if you eat lots of vegetables and salads, with the occasional steak thrown in?

Vegetarian Food for Meat Eaters is not intended to persuade you to become a vegetarian or a vegan, nor is it necessary for you to do so to appreciate the many products I'm going to describe in the following pages. However, in case you're interested, I will suggest some of the many reasons why people decide to remove meat from their diet, how far they go with that, and what you can expect to find when you go out to eat a meal, as a vegetarian, in the UK. But, whatever your day-to-day diet, you're going to discover how you can quickly make and enjoy delicious, healthy meat-based meals without ever using meat.

I'm assuming that you've been lured by the catchy title and have some interest in reducing your meat intake, possibly considering a 'flexitarian' or 'semi-vegetarian diet,' or you wouldn't be reading this short but fact-filled book (easy, Robert). Health issues, weight loss, possible concerns about the way meat gets contaminated with things like hormones and antibiotics, or the environmental impact of eating meat (check it out online: www.thegreenage.co.uk and see what you think), or perhaps you're worried about the way some animals are treated. Maybe a mixture of all of them. Most of all though, I hope you're interested in learning how to eat and enjoy meat dishes and yet technically be a vegetarian. And I'm not talking tofu burgers.

My journey as a vegetarian began over forty years ago with a question: Should I be eating meat? But I think the question now, for all of us, is: Should we be eating *as much* meat as we do? We regard ourselves as omnivores yet have survived because of our consumption of meat (our bodies need vitamin B12, only available from animal sources, as was the vitamin C found in organ meat until we started to eat fruit), but our bodies have evolved since that period in our history when there was little else to eat, and yet we are still eating almost as much meat as we did when we were cave dwellers. Although there has been some reduction in the consumption of red meat in western civilisation recently, you must remember that cave dwellers did their feeding on a feast or famine basis. Now, our meat supplies, in the west, are constant and relentless and therefore, arguably, we do overfeed on them. Originally, we needed the fat, protein, vitamins and minerals, found in the blood and flesh of creatures, to heat and power our bodies and to survive. Is that still the case?

Around ten thousand years ago, during the Neolithic period, we began to move away from the hunter-gatherers' practice of killing prey (instead of scavenging the remains left behind by predators) and began what is known as Agriculture and Settlement, or food crop cultivation and the domestication of animals, gradually introducing wild barley and oats, root vegetables, tubers, and more fruit into our diets. Linseed, chickpeas, peas, and lentils and other plant foods came later. As a result of these changes in diet, our intestines grew longer to process the vegetarian food stuff as well as the meat, so that maximum nourishment could be extracted and absorbed by the body before naturally saying goodbye to it.

So, here's the crunch: the human intestines are between seven and thirteen times longer than our torso. The intestines of all carnivores - lions, tigers, hyenas, etc. - are only three to six times the length of their torsos, to enable protein, fats, and bones to travel through their systems before they putrefy, and the toxins absorbed. What happens to the meat we humans eat? What is the transit time of, say, a steak passing through our systems? Well, the small human intestine is about 6 metres (20 feet) long and the large intestine is 1.5 metres (5 feet long), so 1 to 4 days, with the bulk of the digestion spent in the colon.

And there's more: Homo sapiens - that's us - don't have claws, but they are a sure sign of a carnivore. Horses, elephants, cows, giraffes and buffaloes, as herbivores, don't have or need claws. We have short, flat teeth with canines to eat fruit and raw vegetables, rather than the long, sharp teeth of carnivores, but we can also use our canines and incisors to process cooked meat. Our saliva contains enzymes that begin the digestive process of carbohydrates as we chew, but carnivores' saliva doesn't. Our small intestine secretes sucrase, an enzyme that aids the conversation of sugar to glucose and fructose for our brain and cells. All herbivores masticate and chew sideways, as we do, but carnivores' jaws are designed to work only up and down - tear and swallow. And no respectable carnivore ever suffered from Atherosclerosis (clogged arteries). Not with their short intestines and super-efficient food transit.

We have evolved to a point where most of us no longer needs to hunt and kill our food, hence the rising number of vegetarians and vegans who thrive on plant food, although the latter should be careful to supplement their diet with vitamins B12 and D, and selenium and iodine. The following meat replacement products in this book all contain the nine essential amino acids that humans can't manufacture, plus the vitamins and minerals found in meat. Should we really be eating as much meat as we do?

Does your idea of taking days off from beef burgers and pulled pork involve eating masses of nut roasts, beans, lentils, and tofu, or subsisting on 'rabbit food' (actually, a lot of people are happy doing this, Robert)? It could be that you want to have one or two days a week without eating meat but are worried that a jacket potato with baked beans and grated cheese, or an omelette and chips, will eventually become boring, week after week. Don't think about it, because it's not going to happen. The following pages will show you that you can eat meat dishes, using your own recipes (if you have them) whenever you wish, without harming any creature, and you'll enjoy using and eating meat substitutes that you probably aren't aware of, quickly and with no fuss. Reducing your meat intake is a choice that does not involve a contract or binding promises.

There is a new movement of 'reducetarians' (reducetarian.org) whose members don't follow an all-or-nothing diet like vegetarians and vegans but who are committed to eating less fish, flesh, and fowl (to use my words). There are flexitarians, or vegivores (theflexitarian.co.uk) who eat a plant-based diet with occasional meat, eggs, and dairy, (Isn't that cheating, Robert)? No. That's being practical or 'utilitarian,' as they would say. It's a very interesting website. They mention health, animal welfare and environment as motives for reducing their meat intake, which should, they suggest, be from organic or free-range sources. They advise, initially, committing to one meat-free day a week and calling it something like Meat-Free Monday. In their recipe section, however, there isn't a single dish - even the slow cooker lasagne - that features meat substitutes, so even people who readily admit that they eat meat, as well as vegetarian and vegan food, seem unaware that they could use meat substitutes instead.

Unfortunately, the days are not quite behind us when a vegetarian goes to a restaurant and finds not a single meat- or fish-free dish on the menu. Though there is offered, as a goodwill gesture, a 'nice salad' or a plate of vegetables, or possibly a stir fry (containing no protein, not even a nut or a bean!) at the same price as the meat and fish dishes. Recently, I could have paid £10.50 for some mushroom risotto, £12 for a small bowl of broccoli and pasta in a cheese sauce, and £14.50 for a plate of grilled Mediterranean vegetables in an olde worlde pub in Kent! More about that later. A couple of days ago I stopped off at the Maidstone Motorway Services on the M20 and, just out of curiosity, asked a server at the RoadChef main food and beverage outlet what vegetarian cooked breakfast was on offer, as there was extensive signage for the various breakfasts containing meat, but no mention of a vegetarian option. She immediately listed fried eggs, a Linda McCartney soya sausage, baked beans, mushrooms, and fried tomato.

In the conversation that followed, it turned out that she had several meat-free days a week, eating mainly eggs, jacket potatoes, soup or a cheese salad, but when I asked her if she had ever considered using Linda McCartney sausages herself, or perhaps Quorn Mince, advertised extensively by triple Olympic champion Mo Farah, she shook her head. When I asked why not, she just shrugged her shoulders. This reminds me of people who don't bother to switch banks, car insurers, or energy suppliers, when it could be possible to save money and maybe get better customer service.

Even the French are being urged to say 'non-merci' to foie gras, and to swap their steak-frites for Puy lentils, more vegetables, more wholefoods, and they appear to be listening. Acting upon recommendations by Pascal Canfin of the World Wildlife

Fund France, the French Food & Health Safety Agency is advising that their animal intake should be substantially reduced and red meat, in particular, to five portions per week. The Association Végétarienne de France reports that in 2008 they had 500 members, but today they have 5000. The same trend is happening in Germany, according to the German Vegetarian Union. More than ten per cent of Germans now avoid meat, compared to one per cent over ten years ago, and people are increasingly doing so because of animal welfare and health issues. But they do like their pig: more than half their meat consumption includes pork.

So, I think here would be a good place for us to start to look at the numerous meat substitutes on offer, both in the past and now, which we can use to continue to enjoy meat-based dishes that don't impact the planet or animals and are, in many ways, a far healthier option. And usually cheaper. Don't be like the people who think that meat substitutes are pointless, saying that if you want something which looks and tastes like meat, just eat meat. Missing the point, I think. Several points, actually, the main one being don't kill anything unless your survival depends on it.

And just to be clear about it, the products I mention in this book are ones I have used for years, with some newer ones added recently as I've discovered them, and I reference them because they are convenient and easy to source. I don't get paid to endorse anything by anybody, and I have never asked for any help. I sincerely believe that it's possible to eat a healthier diet based on plant protein, additionally taking advantage of the protective nature of phytonutrients and yet still enjoy meat dishes, using the huge advances in meat replacement technology. That's why I've written this book. So, let's begin in 1974, when I decided to become a vegetarian. Don't yawn. It's interesting.

I thought I'd try it for a while, to see what would happen, despite being an enthusiastic carnivore, possibly addicted to tinned Fray Bentos steak and kidney pies. I stopped eating meat in all its forms (no flesh, fish, or fowl) and relied on eggs, cheese, baked beans and milk for my protein requirements. I developed swollen ankles, which my doctor blamed on my avoiding a 'proper, sensible diet.' I had no idea what to do about it other than to take his advice, although it seemed, somehow, a cop out and not in my nature at all, so I continued with the fried eggs, boiled eggs, omelettes and cheese on toast. Then a strange thing happened.

At this time, I was working as a night switchboard operator in a hotel in Belgravia, so that I would have the days free to pursue my passion for singing and writing songs. One night, with absolutely no warning, I had an intense craving for meat. The need to chew something fibrous was so overpowering I couldn't get it out of my mind. I went in to the main kitchen, deserted at that time, and spotted four plates of food in the chilled display cabinet, three of which were intended for the other night staff, containing two lamb chops per plate. Without hesitation, I ate all six, and savoured every textured morsel, then had to page the night manager to confess my crime. He was very understanding, and was able to replace them, but he did suggest that I consider exactly what had caused the craving or, the next time, I could get in to trouble. I did think I might not be vegetarian material because the craving continued, but I also realised that if I could find something with the texture and, if possible, even the taste of meat, I would be satisfied and still in a job!

This conflicting attitude has travelled with me over many years, because people (especially vegetarians, the most self-righteous of any group I know) challenge me for eating a vegetarian sausage or burger that has the appearance of meat. How could a true vegetarian condone such a thing? The answer is by not eating anything that has died, either by slaughter or from old age, which eventually turned in to the phrase, 'I don't eat anything with a face.' But I do like vegetarian meat. And all the dishes that go with it.

So, the problem, clearly, was that some of the recipes I had used and then embellished over the years, required minced beef. It's the key ingredient in a Bolognese sauce, whatever else you add to the sauce. Chilli con carne, with or without kidney beans and tomatoes, still needs the carne. Shepherd's pie uses minced lamb, and cottage pie needs the minced beef, and so on. I can't remember what prompted me, but I paid a visit to a local health food store, expecting to be told that I should replace the meat with 'beans and pulses,' not even knowing what pulses are (pulses are the dried edible seeds of eleven plants in the legume family, Robert). But, instead, the sales assistant took me to a shelf full of meat-free products, where the main ingredients were textured vegetable protein (TVP) and Textured Soya Protein (TSP) in various forms: mince, chunks, steaks, and some with ham, pork and beef flavouring, made from yeast. The significance of this achievement was that the premium quality protein extracted from soy beans was then extruded in to a spongy mass *similar in texture to meat*, which could then be formed in to any shape you wanted. Its absorbency also meant that it would soak up the taste of whatever sauce it was added to. It was exactly what I was looking for. I bought bags of the stuff and rushed home to try it.

It was awful; the taste was what I imagined old, soggy cardboard would have if a cat had peed on it, and it was the same with the mince and the 'steaks.' The instructions said to rehydrate the stuff in warm water, then add to the sauce, but I eventually found out from others who had tried the stuff that this didn't work and was a common result never to be tried again! Thinking it through, however (in my teens I had trained to be a chemist), it struck me that I was missing the point: meat doesn't just contain protein and water, which I could replace. It also has fat, blood, salt, and sugar as taste factors. A visit to my local library (no internet in those days!) revealed this:

In the early twentieth century, Louis-Camille Maillard, a physician and chemist, was studying the reaction between amino acids and sugar and discovered that meat develops its flavour during the browning stage of cooking, when the sugars in the blood combine with the meat's protein, responding to heat as the catalyst. Bread, biscuits, and virtually everything baked in an oven or fried in a pan is subject to this reaction. It became known as the Maillard reaction. The fat attached to the meat also contributes to its flavour, and marinades containing oil, wine, and lime or lemon juice or vinegar are often used to tenderise the meat and assist penetration of the flavours. Now I knew what was missing: fat and plenty of seasoning. And blood.

For the next batch of textured soya chunks, I prepared a half-pint of warm water, a teaspoon of yeast extract (Marmite is arguably the most popular brand, but most supermarket chains sell their own), a 'borrowed' level teaspoon of Maldon sea salt (it belonged to a delightful young woman who was renting a room next to the communal kitchen in the house where I lived), and a tablespoon of sunflower oil, leaving them to soak for about forty-five minutes. In the meantime, in some Trex or Cookeen (this was 1974 and I thought it would provide the meat fat), I sautéed onions, carrots, potatoes, some quartered chestnut mushrooms and a generous squirt of tomato ketchup, (for sugar and flavour), then added water and the reconstituted chunks and simmered everything on a low heat for about an hour, adding tinned peas and white pepper shortly before serving.

Well, the stew was pretty good. The texture of the soya chunks was excellent, and for me to be able to chew something meaty, that had a savoury flavour and the appearance of meat made me realise what being a vegetarian actually meant to me: I wanted meat dishes but without the meat. This was now possible with TVP prepared with the right elements to make it seem like meat. But I had to wait almost twenty years, until the early nineties, for mycoprotein, a food-grade protein developed from a fungus called Fusarium venenatum, thanks to Marlowe Foods, which had just started manufacturing and distributing Quorn products.

The mycoprotein is bound together using egg albumen and can be fashioned and flavoured to imitate diced chicken, chicken fillets, meatballs, mince, burgers, sausages (that look and taste like sausages and not rolled up mashed potatoes, peas and carrots!), bacon, gammon, steaks, steak strips, and many other products. Because of the egg white they aren't vegan, but Marlowe Foods has introduced a vegan range, using potato protein as the binder, thus making it acceptable to vegans and anyone who happens to be allergic or intolerant to eggs. And the texture is so close to that of meat it's sometimes impossible to tell the difference, particularly when using Quorn mince in a pasta or chilli sauce. The Quorn products do, however, need a few herbs, spices, seasoning and oil to reproduce the taste of meat (so does meat!), but once you've tried them you'll realise that you can use your own recipes or those from a book, or found online, without having to visit the meat section of your local supermarket or butcher. I will say that Quorn's chicken nuggets, fillets and chunks (they sometimes call them pieces, but they're chunks) do taste like chicken without any need to season them, and if you like Coronation Chicken, which I recently re-discovered, just defrost the chunks, mix with mayonnaise, mango chutney, curry powder, and the juice of a small lime, and by some miraculous alchemy you have this outrageous and sublime chicken delight without the dead chicken! It's one of the recipes, found later on in this book.

In chapter one I will be suggesting a list of products to have in your food cupboard and freezer to provide the seasoning necessary to get the best out of the meat substitutes and to save time, bearing in mind that Quorn and the new textured soya protein (TSP) products cook very quickly, and with some, it's just a question of warming them up as they say 'Hi' to the sauce. They're perfect for the 'I want it now' ethos in our lives today. It's a good idea to have the right ingredients to hand, with some time-saving suggestions to get the food on to your plate quickly and hassle free. For instance, by using frozen diced onions, or even a soffrito (diced celery, carrots and onions), as the Italians call it, which supermarkets are now providing in their freezer cabinets, with tinned tomatoes and Quorn or TSP mince, it's possible to make and bake a lasagne in 50 minutes or a perfect Bolognese sauce in twenty minutes!

Chapter One

REPRODUCING THE TEXTURE AND FLAVOUR OF MEAT

The meat replacement business is divided into two parts. There are the basic components, with which you can make your favourite meat dishes using TSP or Quorn Mince to make say a cottage pie or a Chilli Con Carne, or Quorn Chicken Style Pieces or Fillets, (gluten-free), which you could use in a curry or a chicken and leek pie. Then there are the meat-free products which are already formed, such as sausages, burgers, bacon-style slices, gammon-style slices, sausage patties, savoury pies, steak slices, Swedish-style meatballs, escalopes, Crispy Fillets, chicken nuggets and the 'roasts,' which are baked and sliced like joints of meat. The list is pretty extensive, as you'll see, and most of the components and formed products are made and distributed by Quorn and by Linda McCartney Foods, whose Mozzarella quarter-pound burgers, although made from TSP, are the nearest in taste and texture to meat you will find, apart from Quorn Beef Steaks, which I discuss at the end of chapter five. Hardly rabbit food, is it?

Amy's Kitchen and Fry's Foods are long-established companies that tend to specialise in vegan and organic meat-free products, which are now easier to find. I recently discovered Amy's Kitchen gluten-free products in Sainsbury's, Asda, Tesco, Morrison's and Waitrose. The health and wellbeing retailer Holland & Barrett and Morrison's stock Fry's Foods. The major supermarkets do have their meat-free ranges, which are made from (TSP), but whose texture seems a bit rubbery to me, although friends who eat meat tell me that the firmer texture is closer to that of minced beef than Quorn Mince. All these products are available either frozen, chilled, or both, and are found in the vegetarian sections of the supermarkets. However, they can be called something like Healthy Eating, Healthier Living or Free From. The signage is not consistent, and it can be difficult to locate vegetarian and vegan products, so I suggest you ask a member of staff to direct you to the section you want. They will usually take you there! Because of the size supermarkets have grown to, I'll say where you can find them buy adding (frozen) or (chilled/frozen) or (chilled/end-of-aisle) immediately after the product name. I make a point of specifying whether or not a product is suitable for vegans and those who are gluten intolerant, an important consideration when choosing to use a meat substitute. They also contain small amounts of sugar, and people with type 1 diabetes should check the ingredients, in case they need to adjust their medication.

Whatever meat replacement you use, and I'm going to use a 300g bag of Quorn Mince as an example, in order to get the taste right, you are going to have to make some adjustments because of the lack of blood and animal fat, as we discussed in the introduction. If you have ever fried 300g of minced beef you will have been surprised at the amount of saturated fat creeping up the side of the pan, unless you buy very lean mincemeat, and yet a 300g bag of Quorn Mince (chilled/frozen) contains just six grams of unsaturated fat. (Quorn states on their website that 'Quorn spaghetti Bolognese is 90% less fat than a meat version.)

For the missing fat I cook with extra virgin olive oil and/or butter all the time, although the celebrity chefs say it's 'too strong.' It can be peppery, but as you're going to add some pepper to your sauce, what does it matter? And it's a monounsaturated oil (around 76%), which isn't significantly altered when heated (depending on which report you read!), as other oils are, particularly sunflower and corn oil, which oxidise and produce high levels of aldehydes, linked to heart disease and cancer. It was also used by my Tuscan grandmother the whole of her life, and she died at the age of 92.

The 300g bag of Quorn Mince per 100g (which is 3.5 ounces) contains 14.5g protein, 0.9g of salt and 1.8g of sugar. The salt I use is fine sea salt, which I find is more controllable than the rocky stuff, which is good for salting a big pan of water for

pasta. Lately, I've started using reduced-sodium salt (49% of the sodium chloride is replaced by 51% of Potassium Chloride) and I like it. Much healthier and tastes good. However, if you are seasoning a meat-style sauce, you may as well use celery salt and get the added benefit of a flavour I feel should go in to every savoury dish. Also, my source reading on the Maillard reaction invites me to believe that some six hundred components contribute to the flavour and smell of beef cooking, so in this situation, every little helps.

Yeast extract has an intense, savoury taste but comes with its own supply of salt (in some brands the salt content has been lowered) and is a flavouring to add towards the end of the cooking period when everything is ready, and the flavours have combined. Use sparingly. It should just add to the overall taste and not feature at all.

There is some sugar in animal blood, although blood sugar is lower in ruminants (cows, goats and sheep) than it is in monogastric creatures like pigs, horses and rabbits, so it's worth adding a little at a time. A squirt of tomato ketchup will also give extra flavour, and the small amount of sugar involved shouldn't really compromise diabetics. All tomato products contain lycopene, an antioxidant that helps to ward off cancer, although it's more 'bio-available' in ketchup than in fresh tomatoes. If you're using onions in your cooking, remember that browning them will involve some degree of caramelisation and will make them sweeter. This may be all the sweetness you need in a mince-based sauce. It's worth mentioning, in a country where most of us eat far less fibre than we should, that Quorn Mince contains 5.5g of fibre per 100g. All the meat-replacement products are a source of fibre.

So, let's be clear: we're trying to imitate the taste of meat (a mere six hundred components!) and the texture, so we can at least be grateful that the job of texturising has already been achieved by the manufacturers and already has a decent taste. We really just need to concentrate on that taste. This is obviously where herbs and spices play their part, because whatever meat you normally use in your recipes can be bland without some flavouring. Herbs, beef or chicken stock, onions, garlic, celery, salt, and spices such as paprika, cayenne pepper, black and white pepper, and chillies, they all combine with the meat or meat-replacement to provide the overall effect you're trying to achieve. There are, however, some tricks to save time and effort to get the desired effect with your meat substitutes. I'm sure you will have your own tips but here are mine, with a list of dried herbs and spices that form the basis of most of my recipes.

> Basil
> Bisto Onion Gravy Granules
> Bisto Vegetable Gravy Granules
> Bisto Cheese sauce Granules

Black pepper
Celery salt
Chilli powder, hot
Garlic granules
Diced onions - frozen
Herbes de Provence
Italian seasoning
Knorr Aromat (all-purpose savoury seasoning)
Knorr Vegetable Cubes
Knorr Vegetable Stock Pots
Onion granules
Oregano
Oxo Vegetable Stock Cubes
Paprika, hot
Paprika, mild
Reduced salt yeast extract
Sage
Sea Salt, course
Sea Salt, fine
Salt, reduced sodium
Smoked garlic granules
Soffritto, or Vegetable Base Mix (diced white onion, carrot and celery), frozen
Thyme
White pepper

You'll use some of these items often and a few only occasionally. They're all you really need, no matter what you cook, and all can be bought in any supermarket for around a pound, but the amount of oil, salt and sugar you add to the mince and chicken substitutes will depend on what you're used to in your own recipes, your tastes, and your individual health concerns. Some experimentation is essential, and also enjoyable, but I suggest trying my recipes to start with. You won't go wrong. Remember that with meat substitutes there are certain elements missing, which you have to replace, otherwise they will taste like meat substitutes, not like real meat.

Chapter Two

USE TIME SAVERS
AND YOU'RE LAUGHING

Another important element I suggest in this book is that you take advantage of the many time-saving products that are available and don't feel guilty doing so. It took a long time before I wanted to develop any culinary skills other than the very basic, day-to-day activities necessary to avoid starvation. For those whose cooking skills are in their infancy, I have to say that mine got quite School of Fancy over the years but now have moved to School of Better Things to Do, which is why I use frozen, prepared vegetables and garlic and onion powder extensively. The food is still fabulous. I have spent a lot of time, over many years, preparing and cooking meals. I used to cook Christmas dinner for ten people in July, simply because I enjoyed the meal so much. (Were there presents, Robert?) Of course. But now I don't want to spend four hours preparing and baking lasagne. I want it ready in an hour and a half, and it has to be delicious. (Try my recipe). If you enjoy peeling onions and garlic, dicing, wiping your eyes with a wrist, washing the chopping board and knife and trying to get the smell from your fingers, then please ignore this next bit.

One of the happiest moments of my life (and there have been many) was discovering that Asda has a Scratch Cook line of frozen chopped and diced vegetables, my favourite being their Vegetable Base Mix or Italian Soffritto, a mix of diced carrots, celery and onions, used in Bolognese and other sauces, and they are a great base for a quick home-made soup. And, *and*, Diced Onions! It says on the bag 'No Chopping, No Tears, No Fuss, but they don't mention 'No smelly fingers, No Forgotten Rotting Onions.' Then I found that Sainsbury's and Tesco also provide this service for Busy People Who Cook, and they do frozen peeled shallots - and shredded shallots! Incidentally, it's worth keeping some onions in the fridge if you like a few raw slices in a salad, and for those occasions when a friend sees you pouring diced onions from a bag in to your pan and, with a slight frown, says, 'Isn't that a bit lazy, using onions chopped by a machine?' because then you can hand them an onion and a sharp knife and say, 'By all means do the chopping for me - after all, I'm preparing the rest of the meal'. Then you sit down with a drink and watch. You can find peeled garlic cloves. And cubed or sliced butternut squash. Chopped leeks. But not peeled grapes. Why would anybody want peeled grapes?

Ever since I ventured in to my first Lidl and found glass containers of garlic powder and granules, I have never ceased to use it sparingly in my cooking. I remember my mother telling me that my father had threatened divorce if she ever gave him anything cooked with or containing garlic so being an Italian woman she ignored him and used garlic salt, so that he couldn't see or taste any garlic bits. He loved her cooking, and they were married for over fifty years.

Having read on the internet about garlic powder and granules versus fresh garlic, the main point is the taste and the active ingredient allicin, and both are in the powder. It is uniform, there are no bits to burn, no skins to stick to your fingers. It rubs easily in to seasoned flour, you always have some in stock, and the best reason to use fresh garlic is when split in to cloves and pushed inside a corn-fed chicken with sprigs of rosemary before roasting it. I also discovered onion powder and use it in soups, sauces, dressings, in baked beans (when I add a teaspoon of curry powder to make the beans bang a bit), dips and anything that needs a bit of something or other to lift the taste without having bits of actual onion overpowering things.

All frozen vegetables are frozen as soon as they are harvested, so the nutrients haven't been lost or spoiled over time while hanging around waiting to be bought or used. Bird's Eye Frozen Mixed Country Vegetables, containing broccoli and cauliflower florets, sliced carrots, and peas, can also be added to one of the textured soya minces or Quorn Mince, along with frozen diced onions to make a healthy, tasty base for cottage pie. The supermarkets have their own frozen mixed vegetables, to which I add, snapped in to small pieces, fine green beans (Iceland's are superb and are very good value) and anything in the fridge which needs to be used up: soft tomatoes, dried up mushrooms, a leek I forgot to use in the leek and potato soup - you get the idea.

Frozen mashed potatoes are also a massive time saver and can be tarted up in many ways to taste, whether used as a topping or as an accompaniment to the various vegetarian sausages and burgers we'll be dealing with in the next chapter. Typically, the mash is made up of potato, butter, milk, salt, white pepper, water, and 'stabiliser.' From frozen, you can microwave it, add what you like, and have it on the table in fifteen minutes while you cook the other food. It's a processed food, but aren't we processing potatoes ourselves when we make mash at home? I like to add onion and garlic powder and a knob of the butter that contains small salt crystals. Sometimes, I'll add chopped leeks (you can get bags of them frozen) and grated mature Cheddar cheese (available in 500g bags). I'm sure you have your own time and labour savers, but these are a few of my own, and are a match for the speed of the cooking times of meat replacement products which, in themselves, save preparation time as well. In the next chapter I want to introduce what I call the base products, such as mince, chicken pieces, and steak strips, as well as the 'complete' products like burgers, sausages and Frankfurters, which can be fried then cut up and used in sauces.

Another time and labour saving must is pre-cooked rice. The supermarkets' own brands are marvellous, come in different varieties and flavours - Long Grain, Basmati, Pilau, Mushroom, Mexican, Chicken (vegetarian), and brown. They cost about 50p a packet and can be microwaved in two and a half minutes. There are more expensive brands that cost over twice as much, but I can't tell the difference in terms of taste or texture. Some dishes require sticky rice but, other than that, there is nothing to be gained by cooking rice from scratch except more washing up.

To go with the rice, you'll need my recipe for chicken and chickpea curry, to which you could add cinnamon, cumin, fennel seed, coriander, cardamom, asafoetida, red chilli, fenugreek, garam masala, tamarind and turmeric, which would give it exceptional taste. But you can also look at the ingredients in Tesco Medium Curry Powder: coriander seed, cumin Seed, onion, salt, chilli powder, fenugreek, garlic powder, ginger, paprika, turmeric, cinnamon, black pepper, clove, bay leaf and cardamom. It's an excellent mix, it's already made for you with good ingredients, and it's not expensive, so why not use it? (Now I'm hungry, Robert).

Chapter Three

'ARE YOU SURE THIS ISN'T MEAT?'

During the first twenty-seven years of my life, I ate lamb only once, and even when I went to Italy with my mum and dad to see my Italian relatives, I don't remember eating veal, which the Italians were very fond of. In former Yugoslavia, briefly, I enjoyed liver cooked quickly on a griddle, like steak, and from an early age, I ate just about everything else that moved, including, as a very young child, sheep's brains dipped in egg and seasoned flour and fried, except that I took them off the table when my mum wasn't looking and ate them raw. But I never tried snails! (Oooo, why? They're delicious, Robert).

I imagine that if I was starving, I would reluctantly have to kill whatever was available and eat it for survival but, as I have a choice in the matter, I don't. It really is quite simple. Over the years I've become quite inventive, using my chemist's training and the excellent products now on the market to reproduce my favourite meat dishes. Many of the meat eaters who have tried them had no idea they weren't eating meat. Particularly with the mince.

As I mentioned before, I will list the protein, fat, sugar and salt content of each meat substitute, because I feel it's important to know what you're replacing meat with. Also, TVP and mycoprotein meat replacements contain fibre - usually around 6g per 100g - which is an additional health bonus, as most of us don't eat sufficient plant fibre to maintain a healthy colon. The manufacturers are also careful to highlight the use of wheat and/or barley gluten and milk in their products, for those with reactions to them. Salt and sugar amounts are very low in almost all meat alternatives. I will point out whether or not each product I introduce is gluten-free or vegan.

So, I think we'll continue with the extremely versatile Quorn Mince. It's made from mycoprotein, which contains the nine essential amino acids necessary in human nutrition, which our bodies can't produce. It's developed and manufactured by Marlowe Foods, and you can use it to make a very respectable, even flawless, Bolognese ragu for spaghetti, tagliatelle, lasagne etc., or a sauce for cottage pie or some spicy chilli tacos. The mince can be cooked from frozen or chilled. Chilled, it should be added to a ragu that you have already cooked, taking just a few minutes to heat up or, if frozen, microwave for about two minutes or add to the sauce earlier in the cooking process. The mince is gluten free and high in protein (14.5g per 100g). It also contains 5.5g of fibre per 100g, which you won't get from meat, and the fat, sugar and salt levels are very low. Carbohydrates are present at 4.5g per 100g, of which 0.6g are sugars. It is comfortingly chewy and has a texture as close to minced beef as you (or I!) could wish for. Remember to add a tablespoon or so of extra virgin olive oil to make up for the lack of meat fat. To get you going, you could try it in my 20-minute Bolognese sauce recipe later on in the book.

Quorn Mince is perfect for Chilli Con Carne because of its texture and appearance. It does resemble minced beef! But you also get a very good result using the supermarket chains' minced beef product, made from TSP, which has a chewier texture (is that a word, Robert?) Shut up. When your ingredients are cooked and almost ready, add the mince. If it's frozen, add it 10 to 15 minutes earlier than if it's chilled along with a level teaspoon of yeast extract to give your sauce a good savoury, meaty taste. A squirt of tomato ketchup, some sea or reduced-sodium salt and black pepper should make a delicious and convincing meat alternative. The supermarket chains have their own meat substitutes (usually in the vegetarian frozen section), containing TSP, which are worth trying. As long as you don't overcook them they have a good texture. Like the mycoprotein, soya is also a 'complete' protein, with all the nine essential amino acids the human body can't provide for itself. All the following meat-free vegetarian mince products are high in protein and are found in the vegetarian frozen food section:

Tesco Meat-Free Vegetarian Mince: 454g bags. Vegan, but not gluten-free. Per 100g contains 14.8g Soya protein, 6.6g fat, 5.89 fibre, and 4.8g carbohydrate. Small amount of salt.

Sainsbury's Vegetarian Mince: 500g bags. Vegan, but not gluten-free. Per 100g contains 18.6g of Soya protein, 5.0g of fat, 2.0g of fibre, and 11.07 of carbohydrate. Small amount of salt.

Asda Meat-Free Mince: 454g bags. Vegan, but not gluten-free. Per 100g contains 15.0g of Soya protein, 1.6g of fat, 5.6g of fibre, and 5.9g of carbohydrate. Small amount of salt.

Morrison's Meat-Free Mince: 400g bags. Vegan, but not gluten-free. Per 100g 15.8g of Soya protein, 2.4g of fat, 5.2g of fibre, and 6.7g of carbohydrate. Small amount of salt.

Meat the Alternative Beef Style Mince: 500g Bags. Vegan, but not gluten-free. Per100g contains a whopping 19.0g of Soya protein, 0.2g of fat, 5.0g of fibre, and 6.9g of fibre. Small amount of salt.

Customer reviews are mixed, with some preferring Quorn, and others complaining that it's too much like meat! Asda got good reviews, but one thought the texture was 'weird'. Tesco had no reviews. Sainsbury's had widely varying results, with some customers thinking it had 'great texture and taste' while one thought it 'absolutely vile.' Morrison's rated no better, but Meat the Alternative seemed to be very popular, although there were only six reviews, one of which was three years old and another two years old. But it just goes to show that you have to decide for yourself and that everyone has their own taste. Almost all the reviews were based on making and eating 'spag bol.' One woman from Winchester gave it to her husband without telling him it was Meat the Alternative mince, and he didn't comment. She had used it because she was trying to remove some meat from her diet. She, apparently, continues to use it without his knowledge.

Moving on, Quorn also comes in the form of chicken fillets (vegetarian frozen section) and chicken pieces or chunks, (chilled/frozen) and is the best chicken taste and texture of them all. The protein content is reasonably high at 11.5g per 100g, with 5g per 100g of fibre. Salt, sugar and fat amounts are very low. They do have a chicken-like taste, with a very satisfying 'bite.' The packaging suggests frying the fillets and serving them with a 'creamy pesto sauce,' although I find that you can use just about any sauce, and they're delicious. Use the chunks and mix with mayonnaise, chutney, Madras curry powder and lime juice, and you have Coronation Chicken. It takes five minutes! (Recipe ahead). Quorn also suggests using them in a casserole. I like to use them whole with a cheese and leek sauce. The fillets are also brilliant covered in a spicy salsa or in a white wine sauce. In fact, use them in any of your chicken recipes.

The pieces (they are actually chunks) are found in the vegetarian chilled and frozen sections, and are perfect to use in chicken Korma, Thai green curry or in a chicken and mushroom pie, in a creamy mushroom sauce with rice, sweet and sour chicken, or in a chicken stir-fry. The texture is excellent, and they taste great, but don't cook them for more than 15 minutes. Microwave for a minute if frozen.

Apart from the Coronation Chicken above, try the pieces mixed with cashew nuts, diced onions and black bean sauce and/or Hoisin sauce, with a squirt of tomato ketchup and a dash of dark soy sauce, and serve with Chinese noodles or rice. The latter are available from supermarkets pre-cooked, and are delicious, quality products. Make it even more delicious with the addition of chunks of Oriental Spiced Tofu, made by The Tofoo Co, North Yorkshire, and available in the supermarkets' chilled vegetarian food sections. If you happen to have a vegan in the group you're cooking for, you won't be able to use the Quorn Chicken pieces (or fillets) because of the egg white used as a binder, but you can use the Tofoo Oriental Spiced tofu pieces by themselves. The spicy kick is wonderful, and this is why: apart from 97% tofu, they contain cane sugar, ground black pepper, lemon grass powder, desiccated coconut, garlic powder, ginger powder, red chilli powder, sea salt, ground cumin and mint powder. You can get the Black Bean and Hoisin sauces from supermarkets, but you'll probably have to ask an assistant where they're kept, because they won't be where you think they should be. I'm very grateful to the lady in Security in Ashford Asda for taking me straight to them! There are other chicken-style products, usually made from wheat gluten and textured soya but they aren't easy to find. Muscle Food of Basford, Nottinghamshire and Tesco make vegetarian chicken, but I haven't tried them.

Which brings us to Quorn Vegetarian Steak Strips (frozen). They are what you might expect strips of cooked steak to look like, and when fried with onions, some sea salt, and plenty of black pepper, they are tasty, meaty and chewy enough to deserve the name. Per 100g they contain a generous 14.9 grams of protein, 7.7g of fibre, 1.1g of carbohydrate and 2.8g of fat, and they're gluten-free. The salt and sugar content are negligible. They can be added to your ingredients just before assembling a pie. If you use quartered or halved chestnut mushrooms you could call it a steak and kidney pie. I've also used them in a 'beef' curry, although a baguette or thickly sliced sandwich (Iceland's £1 Sliced Bloomer Loaf!) containing peppery steak strips and fried onions is probably the most satisfying way to eat them (apart from if you were to add some fried slices of green peppers), and it takes just ten minutes to make.

I think the most popular recipes for using the steak strips are in a beef stroganoff and in stir fries. If you want to make it an entirely non-meat day you can replace the beef stock in the stroganoff with a heaped teaspoon of yeast extract dissolved in 500mls hot water. Use more or less according to taste and the amount of stock-to-meat ratio you would normally use. And cook from frozen. They will be ready to eat in about 12 minutes. With stir fries, the recipes are endless, but all require intense heat and are made at speed so, again, be careful to add the frozen strips towards the end of the cooking cycle so that they aren't over cooked and lose their texture.

Now, although we're looking at the basic meat-free products, I want to include Swedish Style Meatballs (frozen) at this point because they do rely on the addition of a sauce or fried onions, like the mince and steak strips. A newish company called Meat the Alternative (MTA Foods Ltd), Quorn and Asda make them. The Quorn product (frozen) uses 50% mycoprotein and an undisclosed percentage of textured wheat protein, with the addition of onion and flavourings. Protein content per 100g is from 12.5g, up to Meet the Alternative's 22.1g, (chilled) with small amounts of salt, sugar and fibre. All cook from frozen except Meat the Alternative. The Asda recipe is extensive compared to the others, although Quorn just says 'Natural Flavourings' on their pack while Asda goes to town with: onion purée, tomato purée, chickpea flour, yeast extract, parsley, garlic purée, onion powder, garlic powder, salt, barley malt extract, dextrose, tomato powder, flavouring, black pepper, white pepper, with 65% rehydrated TSP, onion purée and a 'stabiliser' called methyl cellulose, which is used as a thickener and emulsifier in foods. But the result is that the meatballs are delicious and are a healthy alternative to meat. I haven't tried other supermarket meat free meatballs, but I would suggest that you try the ones on offer where you normally shop.

When you open a pack of Meat the Alternative's Beef Style Meatballs (chilled) they do smell beefy, and, when cooked in a sauce, are delicious. This company knows what it's doing impersonating meat. Their other products: Deli Style Ham, Deli Style Beef, Chargrilled Burgers and Beef Style Mince are also very good. You can buy them at Waitrose, if you can find a Waitrose that stocks them, or online from Ocado. In particular, the beef and ham style slices are spectacularly good (vegetarian chilled section), as they are thicker and more satisfying than any other brand. Made from rehydrated soya protein and wheat gluten, per 100g they contain a generous 22.2g of protein and 3.6g of fat. With small amounts of fat, carbs and salt, they are ideal for someone on a diet. These readings are the same for both beef and ham style slices. A favourite fast-food lunch of mine is two slices of toast containing two slices of Jarlsberg or Emmental Cheese and two slices of Deli Style Ham nuked for 10 seconds. We have had the Deli Style Beef slices for Sunday lunch several times. Warmed up for a minute or so in the microwave oven and served with Yorkshire pudding, seasonal vegetables and gravy, they make a very pleasant lunch and a vegetarian meat eater very happy!

But back to the balls, Linda McCartney's Outrageously Succulent Vegetarian Meatballs (frozen) are indeed succulent, and per 100g contain another generous 15.4g protein, 7.7g of fat, 5.2g of carbohydrates, and small amounts of salt and sugar, and generously high in fibre at 9.4g. They're made from rehydrated TSP and an assortment of herbs. The pack instructions say that they should be placed on a baking tray in a preheated oven at 180/fan and cooked for 16-18 minutes. I did that, and the meatballs developed a firm coating, which made them chewier than they need have been, so the next time I tried my usual method (see below) and they were good. Just make sure you follow the I Can't Believe It's Not Meat rules and replace the naturally occurring fat, salt and sugar in meat. I find that you get a better taste and texture if you sauté the meatballs in oil over a medium heat for about ten minutes, turning frequently to brown them. Add to your sauce and cook for a further ten minutes to allow the meatballs to absorb the flavours. (I think they taste better the day after, Robert.) Just as people like to fry sausages then cut them in half and eat in a sandwich, you can do the same with these meatballs, particularly the Asda product, with the scope of herbs and spices. And, of course, you must eat them with spaghetti and a tomato and onion sauce!

Finally, before we move on to foods that contain meat alternatives, let's look at the available replacements for bacon. There are quite a few, but I have to say that the leathery/rubbery consistency of some of them is disappointing. My favourite has to be the smaller rashers produced by Quorn (chilled), which I prefer to the larger Frozen Bacon Style Rashers. They are Deli Bacon Flavour Rashers with a taste of smoky bacon. They cook quickly and in to a good crisp texture. Protein content per 100g is a great 13.9g, fat is 5.2g, with fibre a healthy 6.0g, and very small amounts of sugar and salt. Other brands are available from Holland & Barrett stores and supermarkets. I've tried Tesco's Meat Free Bacon Style Rashers but found the rashers too thick for my liking, as tasty as they were.

Quorn Meat Free Gammon Steaks (frozen)) are excellent, with a robust texture and taste. They are better cooked from frozen in a large frying pan with your eggs, mushrooms and tomatoes, for a great-tasting and healthy breakfast. Protein content per 100g is a very good 16.3g protein, fat 5.9g, fibre 5.9g, with small amounts of sugar and salt. With the addition of some fried Cauldron Foods Cumberland Vegetarian Sausages (chilled), appearing in the next chapter, and some baked beans, you have the basis for a perfect Full English

Breakfast fry-up! Or a Saturday morning brunch. And with no animals involved, apart from the eggs, and hardly any impact on the planet.

Chapter Four

SAUSAGES and BURGERS
- WHERE'S THE BARBIE?

There are now so many vegetarian sausages to choose from - and I'm discounting those that are made of vegetables and mashed potatoes - that it's difficult to know where to start. But I think it's important to be able to find these vegetarian alternatives easily and consistently, so I'll concentrate on the products available, without hassle, in the supermarkets. Companies like Israeli based Tivall and South African family-run firm Fry's have been producing all manner of superb vegetarian and vegan products for many years, but they're difficult to find unless you discover a Holland & Barrett or other health food outlet that stocks them. However, I recently found out that the Morrison's chain sells Fry's frozen vegan schnitzels and steak pies, or you can order them online from Ocado. Their Meat Free Golden Crumbed Schnitzels, made in South Africa from soya and wheat, really are very good. Per 100g they contain 11.7g of protein, 13.7g of fat, 5.0g of fibre and 16.5g of carbohydrate with a small amount of salt. They come in at just under 200 calories each, so consider what you eat them with.

However, their Meat Free Pepper Steak Style Pies were over-salted and had an odd taste. The instructions to bake them on an oven tray in an oven pre-heated to 200C for 25 minutes didn't work. You're supposed to bake them in their very thin metal dishes for 25 minutes, then remove the foil and bake for a further 5-10 minutes, but I just couldn't get them out of their foil dishes because they were stuck. I burned my fingers trying but, in the end, I just left them in. The pastry is too salty as well as the filling, which I had to discard. I'll stick with Quorn steak pies.

Tivall's outstanding Vegetarian Schnitzels, Cocktail Sausages and Frankfurters (end-of-aisle/frozen) can be found at some Waitrose outlets, particularly at certain times of the year (Christmas and Easter) but the most popular sausage producers are Marlowe Foods (Quorn), Cauldron Foods, and Linda McCartney Foods, with their sausages available at most major supermarket chains, reasonably priced, and very acceptable copies of meat bangers.

Quorn and Cauldron do well-packed, firm Cumberland- and Lincolnshire-style sausages. Cauldron's Cumberland sausages are addictively peppery, great for breakfast and with mashed potatoes and plenty of onion gravy (Cauldron sausages are in the vegetarian chilled section, Quorn's in the vegetarian frozen section). Per 100g they contain 13.5g and 14.00g of protein respectively, 7.0g and 8.8g of fat, with small amounts of salt, but the Quorn Cumberlands have 12g of carbohydrate, and they are very peppery. The Cauldron Lincolnshire-style sausages, although containing plenty of herb and spice extracts, are less peppery. Quorn also makes gluten-free sausages, clearly marked on the carton.

The Linda McCartney sausages (frozen) are made from TSP and have a porky taste and a slightly rubbery texture but are pleasing and satisfying. I found that cooking them in the oven on a pre-heated metal tray for 15-18 minutes from chilled gives the best result. Per 100g they contain a massive 18.2g of protein, 6.0g of fat, 8.7g of carbohydrate, 3.0g of fibre and very small amounts of sugar and salt. The Red Onion and Rosemary sausages have plenty of flavour, have a good bite, and will make you think of warmer climates and make you happy.

I like Morrison's Meat-Free Sausages (frozen). We have them with mashed potatoes, mashed suedes and carrots, peas and gravy. They are delicious and cook from frozen at 200C in the oven in about 15 minutes. Made from TSP, they contain a very good 15.2g of protein, 7.7g of fat, 5.8g of carbohydrate, with 6.1g of fibre, and 1.24g of salt. The recipe intrigues me: it includes onion purée, red onion powder, kibbled red onion, rosemary, ginger, white pepper. An inspired assortment of tastes. Gluten-free and suitable for vegans.

Quorn also does some larger, fatter Best of British or Premium sausages (chilled), which appear to contain a paste that, for me, just doesn't work. Per 100g the protein content is a very decent 15.0g, but the fat is 10.4g, and the sugar is 3.1g and is part of a total 10.4g of carbs, which may account for the unfortunate texture. Wild Garlic and Parsley, in that range, does sound inviting but the pasty texture is a turn off. However, Quorn Sweet Chilli Sausages (chilled) per 100g, contain 11.3g of protein, 6.6g of fat, and just 1.3g of sugar. They have a proper bite, a firm consistency and are deliciously spicy. Their bags of Chipolata Sausages (frozen), slightly smaller than most other sausages, are absolutely wonderful. They are firm, have a good bite, and cook quickly, but they seem to have disappeared. No supermarket seems to stock them anymore, and when I called their Customer Services line they told me they still make them but can't force the supermarkets to stock them. Such a shame, but we found we could order them from Ocado. (How many trucks did that take, Robert?)

If you like Frankfurters - and I do think Tivall's are the best in taste and texture - easier to find are Quorn's packs of four (chilled), which really do taste as good as the meaty ones. They're also gluten-free. Per 100g they contain 13.5g of protein and 14.g of fat, 3.5g of fibre and traces of salt and sugar. You're supposed to simmer them in a little water in their packaging for 12 minutes (from chilled), but I have always removed them and cooked them directly in a little water for 10 minutes, then used the water to make pea and ham soup, with a couple of cans of mushy peas, onion powder, white pepper and a slice of finely chopped Quorn Meat Free Gammon. Place Frank in a long bun with a squirt of ketchup and no one will notice the difference, especially the wee ones. Hot dogs tend to contain pork, beef, chicken, turkey, or a mix of all of them, and have nitrites, high levels of sodium and fat. The veggie ones don't, but they taste real.

The recipe for Linda McCartney's 6 Vegetarian Chorizo & Red Pepper Sausages (frozen) is ambitious, and I really like the taste, but the texture is tough and not for me. They contain 35% of rehydrated TSP and then 34% red pepper, which I feel needs to be chopped up into much smaller pieces, but the mixture of garlic purée, smoked paprika, oregano, cumin powder and rosemary gives a great flavour to them.

Although they're not strictly bangers, I'm going to mention Quorn Sausage Patties (frozen) because they are ingenious and inspired and will lead us into the burger section. Part of the Full English Breakfast scenario, they also tuck neatly in to a breakfast-time English muffin (I've seen you cram two or three of them in to a panino, Robert), with a squidge of either colour sauce. As the pack suggests, they can be part of a midweek meat-free meal, served with some new potatoes or sweet potato chips and peas. Per 100g they contain 12.8g of protein, 4.9g fat, hardly any salt or sugar, and 4.7g of fibre. They fry in seven or eight minutes, turned once, and are yummy (are you on the sauce, Robert?) topped with a fried egg and served with baked beans and slices of tomato. Because they cook so quickly you can also use them as a pizza topping, delicious and healthy, on a margherita. Just brush them with a little oil before they go into the oven. Hopefully the supermarkets will continue to stock them!

Linda McCartney's Vegetarian Mozzarella Quarter Pound Burger (frozen) made from rehydrated TSP are, as I mentioned before, the nearest you can get to a real meat burger. Per 100g they contain a whopping 18.2g of protein, 13.8g of fat (that would be the mozzarella talking), 10.3g of carbohydrates and a small amount of salt. You can grill or cook them in the oven from frozen, turning once, and I suspect that, with the amount of fat they contain, you could chuck them on a barbie for about 15 minutes (frozen) and they would taste even better. Widely available, which can't be said for Meat the Alternative's Chargrill Beef Style Quarter Pound Burgers (frozen). I can find them only in Waitrose, and not every branch seems to stock them. And they go quickly. Again, TSP, which turns chewy if you follow the guidelines and grill them for twelve to fourteen minutes, because the fat content per 100g is just 5 grams. Fry them with plenty of oil for about ten minutes, turning once.

Quorn seems to have the edge with their thick Classic Burgers (chilled) and the slimmer Quorn Meat Free Burgers (frozen) because they both look like meat that has been grilled or fried, and they also have a meaty texture and taste. Made from mycoprotein, they're high in protein, quick to cook, and widely available in supermarkets. And just in case you fancy something spicy, Quorn's Southern Fried Burgers will do the trick (frozen). There's a good amount of chicken-style protein and fibre, with black pepper, cayenne pepper, fenugreek, nutmeg, pimento and paprika adding the pizazz. Cook from frozen in an oven set at 200C fan for 15 minutes then slap it into a bread bun and onto a plate of coleslaw and green leaves. Or you can fry them on a medium heat in a small amount of oil for about ten minutes, turning once. Don't overcook them, or you'll ruin the texture. Very nice with sweet potato chips, and beer battered onion rings and salad.

Chapter Five

MAINS, ROASTS, ESCALOPES, FILLETS, KEVINS

Gathering speed, as we are, let's consider this list of meat-free, meaty products: Quorn Pasties, (frozen), Quorn Vegetarian Chicken & Mushroom Pie (chilled), Quorn Lasagne (chilled), Quorn Cottage Pie (chilled section), Vegetarian Steak Pie (chilled), Quorn Meat Free Steak & Gravy Pies (frozen), Quorn Meat Free Stew & Dumplings (chilled), and the brilliant Quorn Meat Free Steak Slice (chilled), because all can be bunged in to the oven and will be ready within the hour, although some can be eaten as they are and others can be microwaved for seven or eight minutes. (That's not at all confusing, Robert). Just check the cooking instructions. These are delicious, satisfying creations, perfect for a venture in to the meat-free zone without any fuss. And they are widely available in supermarkets. The Stew and Dumplings contain the lightest dumplings I've ever tasted, and the stew is moreish. The Meat-Free Steak Slice, with its beefy and somewhat peppery gravy, is an amazingly satisfying parcel, though keep it in the oven at 200C fan for 10-15 minutes from chilled or the pastry can be a bit soggy.

The Quorn Lasagne and Quorn Cottage Pie are both disappointing. Low in protein, at 4.5g and 4.3g per 100g respectively, there also doesn't appear to be very much to eat in the container despite the 500g labelling on the sleeve. The consistency of the cottage pie seems drier than it used to be, and the lasagne has lost a layer of mince sauce, making the pasta chewier than it should be. I also found the cottage pie sauce salty. I think that it's better to make both from scratch using soya or Quorn Mince. That way you can make them as juicy as you wish and freeze generous portions in airtight containers - if there's any left over. (Please see my recipes for both!)

With the other dishes, you can add some frozen mixed vegetables (I use Iceland Mixed Vegetables containing peas, carrots, green beans, and sweetcorn, and sometimes the Bird's Eye equivalent, if they're on offer) and a jug of Bisto Onion Gravy (perhaps not with the lasagne, though). This reminds me of Quorn Vegetarian Peppered Steaks (chilled), which are gluten-free but not vegan. The packaging says that they're 'deliciously succulent', and indeed they are. Covered in chopped red and green peppers and cracked black peppercorns, it makes for an interesting flavour combination that suggests, perhaps, some rice and peas, or sweetcorn, but are they meaty enough to be called steaks? Per 100g they contain 11.7g of protein, 4.9g of fat, and 5.0g of carbohydrate, with 5.4g of fibre, and 1.3g of salt.

You can fry these over a medium heat on the hob (preferred method), and they're ready in 6 minutes. They are not vegan but are gluten-free and worth a try.

Morrison's Meat Free Kievs (Kevins!) With Garlic Butter (frozen) have a meaty texture, but, despite the title and the ingredients listing garlic purée and garlic oil, I didn't get much of that taste, so I just sprinkled some garlic powder over them. They have a realistic chicken flavour, though, and are made from rehydrated TSP. Per 100g, they contain a pretty good 12.9g of protein, 13.3g of fat, 12.3g of carbohydrate, with 4.2g of fibre, and a small amount of salt. Each Kiev is 267 calories, as you would expect, so dieters take care. They are not vegan or gluten-free. (This morning I watched a repeated episode of Chanel Four's Food Un-wrapped, watching real chicken breasts being mashed together until it was possible for the manufacturer to make six Chicken Kievs from one chicken breast. How inventive is that?)

Quorn Crispy Nuggets (frozen) in 300g bags, have also been called Quorn Chicken Nuggets, albeit meat-free. They look and taste like the real thing and are perfect for dipping and for any other reason you would serve chunks of chicken in a light, crispy batter. I've had them with sweet potato fries and coleslaw as a main meal. They're absolutely delicious. Per 100g, they contain an ok 10.3g protein, 4.2g fat and, understandably, 15.8g

ROBERT LINDOP

of carbohydrate, but with a healthy 9.6g fibre and a small amount of salt. Cook from frozen at 200C fan for about 15 minutes. Even with just a small bowl of tomato ketchup, I could see off the whole bag! (And you've done that without breathing haven't you, Robert?) They go very well with frozen potato wedges and peas (mums and dads!), and the children I've tried them on were either oblivious to the fact that they contained plant protein, or thought they tasted 'really chickeny.' Not suitable for vegans and gluten intolerant.

Linda McCartney's Vegetarian Roast (frozen) is quite robust, tasty, and popular with the vegetarian company at Christmas, particularly with its spiced Bramley apple and pomegranate glaze. It's a perfect Sunday roast replacement or week-night meal. Made from rehydrated TSP, per 100g it contains a satisfying 15.2g of protein, 8.1g of fat, 6.1g sugar, a small trace of salt, and 3.1g of fibre. It's loaded with herbs and spices and widely available in the supermarkets. It is also gluten free. Its partner is Linda McCartney's Vegetarian Beef Roast with Red Wine & Shallot Glaze. Cook from frozen in the oven at 200C fan for about 55 minutes. Both roasts are substantial and full of flavour, with enough protein per 100g serving to satisfy a healthy appetite. This one is not gluten-free. Quorn has a gluten-free Vegetarian Gammon Roast (frozen) made from Mycoprotein. There is a good smoky flavour to it, and it comes as a cylinder covered in a film, which you prick with a fork and roast in the oven at 200C fan for fifty minutes. Per 100g it contains a hefty 17.6g of protein, 4.4g fat, 3.8g carbohydrate, with 0.6g sugar, a tiny amount of salt, and a very respectable 7.6g of fibre. Sliced, and eaten with some apple sauce, you will not miss the pig. The packaging suggests that you can eat it sliced in a salad and in a sandwich. (I think I usually forget any that's left over, it gets pushed to the back of the fridge and ends up being cubed and stirred in to a Winter Warmer Soup with a can of mushy peas, when I scour the interior for bits to not waste. The result is not to be sniffed at. Wait...)

For something lighter, you, or if you have any, your children, might care to try Quorn Meat Free Vegan Fishless Fingers (frozen). Naturally, they will be mercury-free - a lot of fish isn't - and they taste fishy, but disappointingly low in protein at 4.4g per 100g, with 7.1g of fat and a whopping 24.1g of carbohydrate. Just thought I'd mention it. The vegan lines are quickly being rolled out and are now widely available in health food stores and supermarkets. Linda McCartney Foods used to make King Size Fish-Free Prawns, but I think they've discontinued that product. I remember when I opened the bag the smell was quite strong, even though the vegetarian prawns were frozen, and I don't think I ever bought them again because they were too much like the real thing!

If you're in the mood, you could have a go at Linda McCartney's Wonderfully Tasty Vegetarian Shredded Hoisin Duck (frozen). Made from rehydrated textured soya and wheat protein, the protein content is high at 22.6g per 100g. The product can be added to a stir-fry. I have an aversion to stir fries, having been offered so many of them over many years - awful, over-salted piles of sliced vegetables and bean sprouts, containing absolutely no protein. Duck did nothing for me anyway, so I haven't tried this shredded variety. You can find it in most major supermarkets. I found it in Morrison's, Canterbury, as I did the Linda McCartney Vegetarian Wonderfully Tasty Pulled Chicken (frozen), and if you like pulled chicken, it's worth a try.

I hope, by now, you've begun to realise that there is far, far more to vegetarian food than you thought, and should you creep over to the dark side, where you think the lettuce munchers are always busy gorging themselves on nuts and berries, slim and well-nourished, you will actually find many old friends similar to the foods you left behind, artfully made and packaged to be cooked and enjoyed without guilt, or fear of eating cat or rat in what you thought was a frozen meat pie you bought.

Moving on, Quorn has developed their basic chicken fillets in some interesting ways. The Crispy Fillets (frozen), have a light batter coating, which demands an invitation to chips and mushy peas, although the fillet has no fish taste whatsoever. Per 100g the protein content is a satisfying 12.5g, fat is 8.5g, and, with batter involved, an understandable 14.2g of carbohydrate, but it still is a source of fibre of 4.0g. Each fillet is around 192 calories, so you can indulge if you wanted to without worrying.

Then there are Mozzarella & Pesto Escalopes (frozen and chilled), with their crusty breaded coating, suggesting some rendezvous with cooked farfalle or fusilli mixed with chopped olives, cherry tomatoes and salad leaves. Lower in protein at 10g per 100g, with 12.9g of fat and 15g of carbohydrate. With each escalope coming in at 270 calories maybe just the one!

The next Escalope, again Quorn, is their Emmental Escalope (frozen and chilled), with a breaded coating. The Emmental has a nice kick, and the beetroot salad they suggest on their website works well. Classic cheese, tomatoes, rocket, and red onion - what's not to like? These escalopes/fillets cook in a hot oven in 18 or 25 minutes, depending on if they're chilled or frozen, so you could be eating half an hour from turning on the oven.

My all-time favourite vegetarian schnitzel, or escalope, is made by the Israeli company Tivall. It has been around in my consciousness since the eighties. Made from soya and wheat protein, in a crumb coating, they fry in about ten minutes with one turnover, have a slight hint of garlic and onion (due to the powders), and are very satisfying to eat. They seem to go with anything. At 200 calories each, you could, in a pinch, fry them without additional oil. Unfortunately, with the wheat and egg white, they are not vegan or for the gluten intolerant. Per 100g they contain 16.0g of protein, 9.5g of fat, 11.0g carbohydrate, with 4.0g fibre, and only a small amount of salt. Waitrose and Sainsbury's seem to be the best suppliers but check on line. You will enjoy them.

The final part of this chapter I have reserved for yet another Quorn product - I know, there are a lot of them - but they've been doing this for over thirty years. A recent discovery, 2 Vegetarian Beef Steaks (frozen) costing around £2 from Morrison's, has blown my mind! Oven cooked from frozen at 200C fan for 22 minutes, they resembled small fillet steaks and are about an inch thick, with the taste of meat that has been browned in a pan, and with a texture that Quorn, to my knowledge, in the past 15 years, has never before achieved. For a vegetarian who is always on the lookout for meat-like vegetarian products, this is perfection. For a meat eater concerned about leaving behind steak and frites, be assured: no harm shall become you, and there is nothing to worry about. There will be no sense of loss when you can eat one of these fine meat-free steaks. In fact, at 125 calories each, you could polish off both of them guilt free. Per 100g, they contain 16g of protein, 5.2g of fat, 3g of carbohydrate and, yes, a healthy 6.9g of fibre. And the steaks are gluten-free.

As it happened, I had been wondering how I could reproduce a proper goulash, something I hadn't eaten for over 40 years, so I cut four steaks into quarters, browned them, and with the help of some onions, garlic, tomatoes, paprika, extra virgin olive oil, and 150mls of vegetable stock there it was. After 30 minutes simmering in the pan, with a sprinkling of chopped parsley, it was, in short, a wonderment. Or a wonder meat.

Chapter Six

MEATY, FISHY, SALADY, SNACKY THINGS TO TRY

Some of the vegetarian food items in this book can be either a main course or a snack. Linda McCartney's Deliciously Comforting Vegetarian Beef, Mushroom & Spinach Wellington Bites (frozen) are really a snack but watch the calories. Just four of them amount to 214 calories and they are both tasty and filling. Per 100g they contain 7.6g of protein, 9.5g of fat, and 26.3g of carbohydrate, from the pastry casings, and a helpful 3.1g of fibre. Into the oven at 200C (brush them with milk to brown them) and they're ready in about 20 minutes. Vegan but not gluten-free.

I think that Quorn Southern Fried Bites - more or less the same as the Southern Burgers, only in chunks - are dippers, but they can also count as a satisfying main meal. A 300g bag serves 2-3 and cook in a 200C fan oven in 18 minutes. Per 100g, they contain 10.3g protein, 8.1g of fat, almost 20g of carbohydrate, and 3.4g of fibre. Three bites are 203 calories. Not suitable for vegans or gluten intolerant. Quite spicy.

The following two products could be used on a warm, sunny day (as opposed to a very cold sunny day, as I write this). Quorn Vegan BBQ strips (frozen), with a hint of smokiness about them thanks to the smoked paprika and tomato powder, can be used in tortillas, salads and as a pizza topping. The first time I used them, I got side-tracked, overcooked them, and they disintegrated, so watch the cooking time. On the hob, fry from frozen for 6 minutes and no more. Per 100g they contain a pretty good 14.3g of protein, a very low 2.9g of fat, 8.4g of carbohydrate, 6.8g of fibre and 1.4g of salt. They contain wheat gluten, and they are good. I used some smoked garlic granules, which made them even more street BBQ. Y'all.

Quorn Mini Savoury Eggs (chilled) or Picnic Eggs, used to be called Scotch eggs, *I think*. There is a chopped free-range boiled egg filling, which is wrapped in a pinkish vegetarian sausage meat then coated in breadcrumbs. With a long list of spices and herbs they are mouth-watering cold, but even nicer just slightly warmed up or at room temperature. Per 100g, they contain 13.6g of protein, 12.6g of fat, 18.2g of carbohydrate, 4.4g of fibre and 1.1g of salt. If you're going to eat the whole 120g six-pack, take note that it comes in at 250 calories (you've eaten six more than once, Robert), and they contain egg and wheat. Still thinking of that hot, steaming summer's day, I wish that I could say something nice about Quorn Vegetarian Chicken Slices and their Vegetarian

Wafer-Thin Ham (chilled), but I can't. Well, all right, they would look nice on a plate with lettuce, cucumber slices, tomatoes, new potatoes, coleslaw, sliced avocado pear, maybe some beetroot, but they have little discernible taste. Looking at the list of ingredients on the Chicken Slices pack, I see the words 'Natural Flavours'. As it's a vegetarian product, what does that mean?

Continuing the stifling heatwave food choices, I will mention Quorn Roasted Sliced Fillets, which are also ready-to-eat but taste-of-very-little. The dreaded words are on the pack: Natural Flavouring, but of what I can't really tell, so I'm going to jump ahead to Quorn Cocktail Sausages and Quorn Vegetarian Pepperoni. (Chilled).

We use the cocktail sausages at Christmas for pigs in blankets, but they are so much more; ready to eat delicious little morsels that deliver flavour and protein. They are also a satisfying chew. If you're in to baking, they are perfect in Toad in the Hole. Per 100g, they contain 12.9g of protein, 11.8g of fat, 10.3g of carbohydrate, and 5.0g of fibre. There is a small amount of salt as well. They are not suitable for vegans or the gluten intolerant.

I thought the Vegetarian Pepperoni slices were meant simply as an adornment for pizzas, and they work perfectly, but the spice hit and smoke flavourings can be used wherever they're needed. I cooked some fusilli pasta, kept back some of the water, and added to it a little milk, butter, and some cheese sauce granules, then shredded pepperoni and ended up with a delicious pasta carbonara. (I did add a tablespoon of grated extra-mature Cheddar). You can also make a great toasted sandwich of pre-sliced Emmental or Cheddar cheese and pepperoni slices to wake up your taste buds. Per 100g they contain 11.3g protein, 7.1g of fat, 14.1g of carbohydrate, 4.1g of fibre, and just 1.g of salt. They contain free range egg white but no gluten.

Chapter Seven

MY MEAT SUBSTITUTE
TRY-OUT RECIPES

This has been a fairly extensive list of products covering beef, ham, chicken, and fish substitutes for you to experiment with. You will have a good idea of the nutritional values of these and my opinion on their taste, texture, ease of preparation and degree of satisfaction. I realise that I've tended to concentrate on Marlowe Foods' Quorn products, and also the Linda McCartney brand, and that's mainly because they are widely available, and they are good at what they do. I must stress that this is a highly subjective area, and you should try the other respected brands and the supermarkets' own products to decide for yourself which you prefer and which work for you.

Although I originally put this book together for people with their own tried and tested recipes who just wanted to reduce their meat intake without having to resort to nut roasts and tofu (both can be delicious, Robert), I realise that there are people who, with the same motive, haven't yet developed any real culinary skills who need my help. (Remember, at the beginning of this book, I told you I was addicted to tinned steak and kidney pies with no vegetables to speak of? That was in my late twenties!) Also, I've been surprised at just how many people I've met recently who have been influenced by vegetarian or vegan partners, children, relatives and friends - far more than I ever remember - who showed real interest when I explained what Vegetarian Food For Meat Eaters is about. A few years back I would have been staring back at faces filled with pity. So, try these, and see what you think. Constructive criticism and suggestions, maybe a joke or a recipe, are welcome at vegetarianmeateaters@yahoo.co.uk.

20-Minute Meaty Bolognese Sauce (for 2 or 3 Greedy People)

200g Quorn or Textured Soya Mince, frozen

4 tbsp extra virgin olive oil

200g diced onions, frozen

100g soffrito, frozen

1 400g tin of chopped tomatoes

150 mls of hot water, in a measuring jug

1 level tsp each of basil, oregano and fine salt

2 heaped tsp each of garlic granules and onion powder

1 vegetable stock cube (I use Oxo or Knorr or their Vegetarian Stock Pots)

Tomato purée, to taste

Black pepper, to taste

Tomato ketchup, to taste

Directions

> 1. On a medium heat sauté the onions and soffrito in the oil for about seven minutes, or until they have softened
>
> 2. Turn up the heat and add the hot water, herbs, salt, vegetable stock cube, and the

chopped tomatoes and stir well for five minutes

3. Add the mince, stir, and cook for about eight minutes.

4. From start to finish, the sauce takes twenty minutes to prepare and cook and is ready to serve with your favourite pasta. If allowed to stand for an hour or overnight, it tastes even better.

40-Minute Meaty Chilli Con Carne (for 4 Greedy People)

300g Quorn or Textured Vegetable Mince (from frozen)

4 tbsp extra virgin olive oil

200g frozen diced onions

100g frozen soffrito

400g tin of chopped tomatoes

400g red kidney beans, drained (save it for a soup)

300 mls of hot water, in a measuring jug

1 level tsp yeast extract, dissolved in the hot water

2 heaped tsp each of garlic granules and onion powder, dissolved in the hot water

1 tbsp Bisto Onion Gravy Granules (dissolved in the hot water)

1 vegetable stock cube (I use Oxo or Knorr)

2 level tbsp hot chilli powder

1 level tsp medium paprika

Tomato ketchup, to taste

Directions

1. On a medium heat, sauté the onions and soffrito in the oil for about 10 minutes or until they have softened.

2. Turn up the heat and add the chopped tomatoes, drained kidney beans, and the hot water containing the yeast extract, garlic granules, onion powder, and the onion gravy granules.

3. Crumble in the stock cube and the mince, stir, and cook for about ten minutes. Add the paprika and chilli powder and salt to taste. Use the tomato ketchup if you like it sweeter and to soften the chilli kick. Done.

60-Minute Meaty Cottage Pie (for 2 Greedy People)

400g Frozen Quorn or Textured Soya Mince

200g frozen diced onions

4 tbsp extra virgin olive oil

200g frozen mixed vegetables (Bird's Eye or supermarket brand small-cut vegetables)

8 chestnut mushrooms, quartered

300 mls hot water, in a measuring jug

1 tsp each of garlic granules and Herbes de Provence, dissolved in the hot water

2 tsp of onion granules, dissolved in the hot water

1 level tsp low salt yeast extract, dissolved in the hot water

2 heaped tbsp onion gravy granules, dissolved in the hot water

1 vegetable stock cube (I use Oxo or Knorr) or a Knorr vegetable stock pot

Black Pepper, to taste

700g frozen mashed potatoes

Directions

1. Preheat the oven to 200C/fan/gas mark 6 and heat one litre of water in the kettle.

2. On a high heat sauté the onions and mushrooms in the oil for about 8 minutes. Add the hot water containing the garlic granules, Herbes de Provence, onion granules, yeast extract, onion gravy granules, crumbled vegetable cube, and frozen mixed vegetables.

3. Cook for a further five minutes and add the mince. Let the mixture simmer while you microwave the mashed potatoes.

4. Loosen the mash with a little butter and milk to make it easier to spread over the mince.

5. Finally, season the pie mixture to your taste and carefully pour or ladle into an ovenproof (one-and-a-half litre) dish and top with the mash. Bake for 30 minutes until the mash has browned. Sprinkle some grated cheese for extra taste and colour, if you like.

90-Minute Mince Lasagne (for 4 Greedy or 6 Normal People)

300g Quorn or Textured Soya Mince (from frozen)

200g frozen soffritto

100g frozen diced white onion

4 tbsp extra virgin olive oil

2 x 400g tins of chopped tomatoes

200 mls hot water, in a measuring jug

1 level tsp each of basil, oregano, fine salt

2 heaped tsp each of garlic granules and onion powder

1 vegetable stock cube (I use Oxo or Knorr, especially their Vegetable Stock pots))

Tomato purée, to taste

12 uncooked pasta sheets

1 430g jar of white lasagne sauce (I get a good result with Tesco's)

Tomato ketchup, to taste

Black pepper and salt, to taste

Directions

1. Pre heat the oven to 200C Fan/gas mark 6.

2. Heat 200mls water in the kettle or in a measuring jug in the microwave oven.

3. On a high heat, sauté the soffritto and onions in the oil for about seven minutes, add the hot water and the vegetable cube and herbs. Stir a few times then add the tinned tomatoes and the mince. Cook for ten minutes. The sauce, from start to finish, is ready in 20 minutes.

4. Ladle three centimetres (just over an inch) of sauce in to a 1.5 litre ovenproof dish and cover with the pasta sheets. Do the same with the sauce and pasta sheets two more times, finishing with the last of the sauce.

5. Pour the white sauce (give the jar a good shake first) from side to side, and then lengthways, concentrating on filling in the edges. You can put white sauce and grated Parmesan cheese in between the layers, if you wish. I no longer use Parmesan (the Italians insist on using rennet from the stomachs of slaughtered calves to curdle the milk), but a little mature cheddar is fine.

6. Place in the oven on a metal baking tray for 70 minutes or until the Bolognese sauce is bubbling and the white sauce has browned. It's delicious with garlic bread and a crisp green salad.

Meat the Alternative Meat Balls in Tomato Sauce (for Four)

300g Meat the Alternative Meat Balls

4 tbsp extra virgin olive oil

200g frozen diced onions

200g frozen soffrito

2 400g tins of chopped tomatoes

300 mls of hot water, in a measuring jug

2 level tsp each of basil, oregano, and fine salt, dissolved in the hot water

4 heaped tsp each of garlic granules and onion powder, dissolved in the hot water

2 vegetable stock cubes (1 Oxo and 1 Knorr), dissolved in the hot water

1 level tsp low salt yeast extract, dissolved in the hot water

1 level tsp brown sugar

Tomato purée (to taste)

Black pepper (to taste)

Tomato Ketchup (to taste)

Directions

1. On a high heat sauté the onions and soffrito in the oil for about seven minutes, or until they have softened.

2. Add the hot water containing the herbs, salt, vegetable stock cubes, and the chopped tomatoes, stirring well.

3. After five minutes, add the meat balls. Stir, and carry on cooking for about 15 minutes. The meatballs are already cooked, so you're basically warming them up as you're cooking the sauce, and all should be ready to serve in thirty minutes from start to finish.

Coronation Chicken

200g Quorn Chicken Style Pieces, frozen

4 tbsp Mayonnaise

2 tbsp Mango Chutney

1 tsp Curry Powder

Juice of 1 lime

Directions

1. Defrost the Quorn Chicken Style Pieces.

2. Mix together the other ingredients, then add the chicken style pieces and combine them with the sauce. If using fillets, cut them to the required size and stir into the rest of the ingredients.

Chicken and Chickpea Curry (For 2 or 3 Greedy People)

300g Quorn Chicken Pieces, defrosted

3 tbsp extra virgin olive oil

200g frozen diced onions

1 400g tin chopped tomatoes

1 400g tin of chick peas, drained (save the liquor for a soup)

150g chopped fresh cauliflower

400 mls of hot water, in a measuring jug

2 level tsp garlic granules

2 heaped tsp medium hot curry powder

1 level tsp Garam masala

1 level tsp ground cumin

1 level tsp ground coriander

2 vegetable stock cubes (I use Oxo or Knorr or their Vegetarian Stock Pots)

1 tbsp tomato purée

Black pepper, to taste

Sea salt, to taste

Directions

1. On a high heat, sauté the onions in the oil for about seven minutes, or until they have softened.

2. Add the tinned tomatoes, cauliflower, and chick peas, and cook for a further 10 minutes.

3. Dissolve the vegetable cubes, herbs, and spices in the hot water, and pour in to the pan.

4. Reduce the heat and stir in the chicken pieces. Cook for about 30 minutes. (I have added the Garam masala, ground cumin and ground coriander for extra flavour, but just using the mixed curry powder will do. I buy curry powder from Tesco, Sainsbury, and Asda but embellish the result with these added spices to support the chicken-style pieces.)

Chicken, Gammon and Leek Pie

200g frozen diced onions

4 tbsp extra virgin olive oil

200g Quorn Chicken Pieces (from chilled)

2 slices Quorn Gammon, diced

1 jacket potato (300g), diced

300g thinly sliced leeks

4 mini portabella mushrooms, sliced thickly

100g petit pois or peas

500mls hot water

2 heaped tsp each of garlic granules and onion powder

2 vegetable cubes (I use Oxo or Knorr)

6 tbsp Béchamel sauce (white sauce for lasagne)

A generous knob of butter

375g butter puff pastry, ready rolled

Black pepper and salt, to taste

Directions

    1. Preheat oven to 200Cfan/gas 6.

    2. Heat 500mls water in the kettle.

3. On medium heat, sauté the onions, diced potatoes, and diced gammon in the oil for about seven minutes.

4. Turn up the heat and add the leaks, mushrooms, chicken pieces, and the hot water in which the stock cubes, garlic, and onion powder have been dissolved. Stir well.

5. Bring to a simmer. Add the petit pois, white sauce and butter. Stir well.

6. Switch off the heat and cool for ten minutes.

7. Carefully pour or ladle into a 1.5 litre ovenproof oblong dish. Cover with unrolled pastry, making some cuts to allow the steam to escape.

8. Brush with milk and bake in the oven for 35 minutes, or until the pastry is browned.

Ham and Cheese Tasty Toastie

2 slices Meat the Alternative Ham Style Deli Slices

2 slices Mature Cheddar cheese, or Emmental or Gruyere

2 Slices toasting bread (I use Sainsbury's Barley & Oat Bread or Iceland Bloomer)

1 level tbl spoon mayonnaise

A few slices of tomato

Black pepper

Directions

1. Build up the layers in between two slices of toast, then nuke in the microwave oven for 20 seconds. As far as I know, you can only buy the ham-style slices from Waitrose. You could also use Quorn Gammon slices, but you might want to fry them for about five minutes, as they're quite thick. This snack is actually a meal!

60-Minute Steak and Vegetable Pie (For 2 Greedy People)

300g Quorn Pieces (chunks), room temperature

100g Quorn or Textured Soya Protein Mince (from frozen)

3 tbsp extra virgin olive oil

300g frozen diced onions

200g Sainsbury's Basic Frozen Vegetables (or equivalent)

10 small chestnut mushrooms, halved

375g Sainsbury's All Butter Puff Pastry (or equivalent) chilled

550 mls hot water, in a measuring jug

4 level tbl Bisto Onion Gravy Granules (or equivalent)

2 level tsp of garlic granules

1 level tsp celery salt

1 level teaspoon reduced salt yeast extract

1 pinch Herbes de Provence

1 vegetable stock cube (I use Oxo or Knorr or their Vegetarian Stock Pots)

2 level tsp tomato purée

Black pepper, to taste

Directions

1. Preheat the oven to 200C Fan/Gas 6 and heat the water in a kettle.

2. On a medium heat, sauté the onions in the oil for about 10 minutes, then add the mushrooms.

3. Mix the rest of the ingredients in the jug of hot water, turn up the heat, and add to the pan.

4. After five minutes add the Quorn Pieces and add the mince. Stir and simmer for about 20 minutes. Allow to cool for a while. No added salt should be necessary, but some black pepper will bring out the taste.

5. Carefully ladle into a 1.5 litre ovenproof oblong dish, remove the thoroughly defrosted puff pastry from the box, and roll out over the dish. Brush with milk or beaten egg, and bake for 25 minutes. The reason I use Sainsbury's Basic Frozen Vegetables is because the 40% carrots are diced, the 30% cauliflower and the 10% broccoli are finely cut, and there are also 20% peas, so you can hide them all among the chunks and mince and enjoy a healthier, tastier meal.)

Chapter Eight

VEGETARIANS AND VEGANS
NEED TO LOOSEN UP!

You can find more recipes online, particularly from Quorn and Linda McCartney Foods, but you'll hardly ever find vegetarian or vegan recipes that use meat substitutes, as I mentioned before. The majority, instead, feature oatmeal, nuts, beans, lentils, quinoa, chickpeas, tofu, tempeh, seitan and, in one inspired recipe I found, cauliflower florets, pulsed in a blender to resemble cooked rice then 'stained' with soy sauce and sesame oil to look like ground beef! If you wanted to make a meat-free 'Ground Beef Tacos' why wouldn't you just use Quorn or TSP mince?

I think the problem may be linked to vegetarianism itself. We vegetarians, and vegans, are inclined to feel guilty of hypocrisy if we eat anything that looks or tastes remotely like meat. It's quite possible that we are a bit self-righteous - dare I say, a bit smug - refusing to eat anything that looks as if it could have been killed, chopped up, and cooked (although this doesn't really account for the cauliflower subterfuge.) It's as if we're cheating, and are not true to the cause. It was a long time before we would even consider eating anything that wasn't a patty, rissole, or nut cutlet/lentil/mung bean/casserole/stew that, like the unrefined wholemeal brick loaf sawn into slices, could damage or actually break a tooth.

In the sixties and seventies, Cranks, on Marshall Street, just off Carnaby Street in London, set the tone of vegetarianism and veganism, with their wholefood salads, containing amazing and varied ingredients that made you pee all night, freshly baked wholegrain loaves that had to be arm-wrestled to get them in to a bag, and fruit salads that would make your heart sing. It was also a 'look' that insisted you sit at refectory style tables, on uncomfortable, bleached oak chairs, and eat from hand-thrown stoneware pottery, on quarry tiles, surrounded by exposed brick walls.

In the seventies, I used to eat at Manna, the vegan restaurant next to Primrose Hill, when that area housed common people like me, who were mainly actors, writers, artists, and musicians. I'm amazed and pleased to see that it's still open (evenings only). I fondly remember the dirty windows, torn net curtains, chipped crockery, and treacly Muscovado sugar that hardened in the bowls over time, so you had to hack at it with a knife, risking severe injury or amputation. There was no shape or look or taste in the food they served that could possibly ever be associated, in any way, with anything resembling meat.

That blueprint - or should I say foodprint - is so firmly entrenched in our understanding of what it means to be a vegan or vegetarian, that caterers out there are very careful not to offend our sensibilities by providing meat-free dishes that remotely suggest, look, or taste like meat. Perhaps they thoughtfully feel that we would be offended or upset if offered food that resembled meat? To some extent that may be true, but we're not unwise. If Sainsbury's Ashford Café and the Maidstone M20 Services RoadChef outlet (there must be others!) can continue to cook and sell Soya-based sausages without Vegetarian Wrath closing them down, why aren't they available at every catering venue that's happy to take our money? That reminds me of the tweeted outcry after the UK introduced new five pound notes that reportedly contained animal fat. Well, it's in an awful lot products we use, certainly touch, but we don't eat fivers. Do we? I think there's a law against it!

Despite the fact that we're now able to make healthy, nutritionally rich products that look and taste like meat, though made from plant-based protein, fundamentalist vegans and vegetarians have to recognise that eating them is not going to cause them to revert to their carnivore days (or it shouldn't!). Some, like myself, left those days behind almost a lifetime ago, plus the meat-replacement products cost a lot less than the real thing, involve no abuse of animals, and impact on our environment and the planet considerably less. The world's livestock pumps millions of tonnes of methane gas in to the air every year, arguably contributing to climate change, as more and more emerging economies create further demand for the 99p beef burger. Last week, watching the excellent Channel 4 programme *Food Unwrapped*, a farmer stated that thirty-three percent of the cereals we grow in the UK are fed to livestock instead of people. Are we eating too much meat?

It's disappointing that our restaurants, pubs, and cafes are still reluctant to engage with meat substitutes in any meaningful way. A vegetarian friend said to me, when I mentioned the book, that she was not keen on the idea of using meat replacements, although she had really enjoyed a 'meat' pie I once made using Quorn chunks in a port and onion gravy. I've served lasagne to a group of people, that contained what appeared to be minced beef, and the meat eaters loved it, but it freaked out the one vegetarian! But bless our local Sainsbury's Cafe in Ashford, Kent which has a superb extra big vegetarian all-day breakfast, to which they've included two Sainsbury's Vegetarian Cumberland Style sausages (sometimes there are three!), costing £5. I told James, the manager, that it's very rare to find meat substitutes like sausages in catering outlets, and it appears that someone along the chain of command has made the decision to provide them in the vegetarian breakfast. Kudos, whoever you are! You're selling your own goods, and making some vegetarians very happy. As I keep banging on about them, Maidstone Services on the M20 has one Linda McCartney sausage in its vegetarian breakfast (wow!), and a local inn has an entire menu page of vegetarian dishes, including a disturbingly realistic, char-grilled soya burger! I know, that's all I've got, but I hope there are other similar outlets.

The (V) against menu entries are few in restaurants and cafés and are not always vegetarian. Pasta dishes with Parmesan or Mozzarella cheese usually aren't, as they're made from animal rennet extracted from the stomach lining of new-born male goats and calves after they have been slaughtered, and you have to ask the waiter to ask the chef if the cheeses are made with vegetarian rennet. Sainsbury's sells vegetarian Dried Grated Hard Cheese, which is a pretty good substitute for Parmesan and, interestingly, is produced and packed in Italy, and Waitrose does a vegetarian Parmesan-like solid wedge called Quattro Cento. Other cheeses made using animal rennet are Pecorino Romano, Grana Padano, Gorgonzola, Manchego, Gruyere, Emmental, Camembert and Vacherin, although I'm happy to report that Cornish Brie, Danish Blue and Wensleydale supplied by Tesco Stores, are vegetarian, as are the various strength Cheddars. There are others, which you can find out about by visiting the British Cheese Board website but always check the packaging for confirmation that the cheese wasn't made using animal rennet.

Also, the so-called 'Vegetarian Option' soup of the day will often contain chicken or boiled bones stock, although the person taking your order will unwittingly swear that it's a lovely vegetarian vegetable soup. A couple recently interviewed on the BBC1 Rip Off Britain: Food series, were offered lobster risotto as a vegetarian option and, in another venue, a chef sat at their table as they explained that his pasta dishes were, in fact, not the vegetarian options he was offering because the cheese he used in them (Mozzarella) was made from milk curdled by animal rennet. To be fair, I thought that all cheeses sold in this country were now made from vegetable rennet, so it was a shock to discover that they are not.

Eating out in Britain highlights a disappointing lack of knowledge and understanding of what is available to chefs and cooks when catering for people who, for whatever reason, don't want to eat meat and, for vegans, eating out is a minefield. Since the beginning of 2018 there has been a growing interest in veganism here, and many more are joining the 3.5 million in the UK, so what caused it? It may be that people are becoming more aware of the way livestock is treated, and what they're treated with, but that doesn't explain why they want to bypass the vegetarian stage. Marlowe Foods Quorn brand and Linda McCartney

Foods have enlarged their vegan ranges, and the supermarkets are continually expanding their Free From varieties, but the catering industry doesn't appear to have responded in any way other than to adopt their usual dismissive stance; it's not serious; it's just a phase; too frivolous. Well, the Marlowe Foods Quorn brand reported in February this year that global sales rose by 16% last year, with growth in Europe and the US running at 27% and 35% respectively. Marlowe Foods' management expects the business to become a billion-dollar business by 2027. Not bad for a brand that was launched in 1985.

Chefs and food providers, generally, continue to deploy as little time and energy as possible to learning about modern plant-based foods, and the growing public interest in their consumption. They don't seem to care enough to want to try them out. This lack of commitment, in fact complacency, has a comeback: vegetarians and vegans almost always eat out with their meat-eating parents, siblings, partners, friends, relatives and children, and if the vegetarian or vegan can't find anything to eat or doesn't fancy what's on the menu - and there's usually very little to choose from - they all leave and try elsewhere. The lack of choice is appalling, and we are getting fussier about what grudging token gestures we're prepared to accept, because most of us are aware of the simple and satisfying dishes which can be achieved with the Mycoprotein and Textured Soya Protein products you've been reading about in this book. Pea Risotto, a stir-fry or a vegetable pie, charged at the same price as the extensive list of meat, chicken and fish dishes on the same menu, won't do.

Of course, it isn't helped by the fact that there isn't a single TV chef that will be seen to be using mycoprotein and textured vegetable protein. Not to my knowledge, anyway. Maybe they feel it's beneath them, but look at their training: years of working sleep-deprived long hours in hot, sweaty kitchens, dismembering and cooking small animals whilst being screamed at by chefs, has to be a form of brain washing, and if that background says you have to work with bloody minced beef to prepare a dish, how likely are you to believe that using a 500g bag of textured soya mince instead is acceptable? There's nothing to brown, no provenance of the meat to consider, no concern about its tenderness, just some flavours and herbs to combine, so there is no skill involved to show off. Except that if you don't add the right ingredients, the right flavourings, in the right amounts, and cook for the correct length of time, the food will not taste good, people will say it tastes 'funny' and artificial, so you have to work harder to get it right, or it's back to killing and cooking livestock. Such a shame that one of them hasn't the vision to engage with the products on TV. They would probably work up to attracting another million or so viewers.

So, now you know you can reproduce virtually any meat dish and it's still vegetarian. Hence my suggestion that a meat eater can also be a vegetarian, you *can* have your cake and eat it, just don't expect to find it in catering outlets in Britain. Or on TV. You'll have to do it yourself.

Chapter Nine

THE MAGIC OF HERBS AND SPICES

I use this rather silly title because my first obsession in Life was with chemistry, and it's still a subject that fills me with awe. The reason we came in to existence, everything we do, everything around us, and the circumstances which will, eventually, cause us to cease to be, is the result of interactions between substances.

Think of an egg, which you are going to fry in butter, which has been heated up in a pan. Look at it as you crack the shell and release it. Watch it change texture and colour. And taste. Slide the egg on to a slice of toast, the bread having changed colour and texture in the toaster, following the Maillard reaction I referred to in the introduction. Sprinkle some sodium chloride (ok, salt) on to it and maybe a half grind of Piperine (ok, black pepper), then start eating your egg on toast. Amylase, an enzyme in your saliva will begin to react to the carbohydrate (ok, starch) in the bread, beginning the digestion process, causing it to taste sweeter and eventually breaking it down in to maltose. Wouldn't you call that magic?

The rather lengthy list of herbs and spices I suggested to you in Chapter One is just pure chemistry for you to use in your cooking, and is part of the process of change we indulge in every day. If you examine the packaging containing the meat substitutes we've been discussing, you will note that the ingredients can be quite extensive, and there will be items such as 'firming agents' or 'gelling agent's or the ubiquitous Methyl Cellulose, used as a thickener and emulsifier. Some products, like those I have discussed in previous chapters, will also have a long list of included tastes - remember Asda Meatballs comprising this lot: Onion Purée, Tomato Purée, Chickpea Flour, Yeast Extract, Parsley, Garlic Purée, Onion Powder, Garlic Powder, Salt, Barley Malt Extract, Dextrose, Tomato Powder, Flavouring, Black Pepper, White Pepper? And this is where absolute knowledge of the magical herbs and spices in your dark cupboard is so necessary to have, because it is a sad truth that add just *one* wrong herb or spice that shouldn't be in whatever you're cooking, and people will want to spit it out. They will pretend that they aren't really hungry, or a bothersome tooth is hurting when they eat, and they may even fake a heart attack to get out of eating the disgusting food you're trying to POISON them with. So, get to know the tastes and how to use and combine them like a good chemist, and note when something doesn't work and try to figure out why. All savoury tastes should work together as a team, with nothing stealing the spotlight except, perhaps, chilli. And these tastes are perfect for meat substitutes which, though they have already been flavoured, to some extent, by the manufacturer, are a blank canvass and can be coaxed to further resemble the meat they're trying to be.

Most of the list is self-explanatory: salt, pepper (white pepper is hotter than black but is less complex than black pepper and should be used where you don't want it to be seen), stock cubes, chilli powder etc, but you have to be careful with certain herbs that need to be used sparingly. Thyme is wonderful and aromatic yet quite strong, so add pinch by pinch (PBP). Some people use the 'Italian' herbs Basil and Oregano together in the same dish, as I once did, but now I like to use them separately, in a meat-free diet. I would sprinkle Oregano (I grow it in a massive pot) on to a pizza, and fresh Basil has to be with vegetarian Mozzarella, big fat tomatoes and extra virgin olive oil. Together, maybe in a lasagne.

I discovered Herbes de Provence about eight years ago, and I suggest you try it PBP in stews, and soups, very sparingly. It is a wonderful cocktail of tastes and smells. Nobody will know what it is, and they will be annoyed at how clever you are, particularly if you sprinkle it on a dish of mixed vegetables and olive oil, with large chunks of onion and whole garlic cloves, before they go in to the oven. The fragrance coming from the oven will knock your socks off and linger in your bedrooms for days!

Knorr Aromat is to be used only in an emergency, typically when you've been adding this and that from the dark recesses of your fridge, to boost your food recycling profile, and ended up with something that tastes of nothing, with an edge towards gardening compost. Whatever the delinquent dish, add a heaped teaspoonful of Aromat and a squirt of tomato ketchup. All will be fine because Aromat contains monosodium glutamate, a flavour enhancer, and partially hydrogenated palm fat which, normally, I wouldn't go anywhere near. It contains wheat starch, a no-no for those with gluten intolerance and lactose, so it's not vegan. As I say, only in an emergency! A safer redeemer would be Knorr Vegetable Stock Pots. Vegan and acceptable to gluten intolerant, one tiny pot will turn a failure in to a warm, glowing sauce, soup or whatever. And much more benign. You don't want a dinner guest or someone you're trying to impress suddenly turn purple and gasp, between dying breaths, that they're allergic to MSG.

Now, I know the granules on the list are not an herb, nor a spice, but they provide flavour and thickening powers, so are perfect for sauces. A cheese sauce to hold together vegetables and pasta, and to make macaroni cheese, and the onion gravy granules in anything savoury and brown you're going to cook in the oven. Also, for making gravy.

Celery Salt is, I believe, something that should go in to anything savoury. I think of celery as a beautiful, unusual voice that the choirmaster places in the middle, towards the back, of a group of competent singers, making an entirely richer, fuller sound. Of course, you can buy celery seeds, which are preferable, because we really don't need more salt in our diet. We could even buy celery and chop it in to tiny pieces, but we don't do that (see chapter two and below). Just make sure you can't tell it's there unless you're making a celery soup, or a thick vegetable soup, where you want that taste to come through.

My final entry is the Soffritto mix I keep banging on about, the clever combination of chopped celery, carrots and onion used a lot in Italy as the basis for many of their dishes, but also active in Spanish, Portuguese and Latin American cooking. You can make a large batch of Soffritto and use it to make four different dishes quite easily. Mix it into anything you want to enrich and make healthier, including soups, omelettes, and any of the meat-substitutes, remembering that some six hundred components contribute to the flavour and smell of beef cooking!

Chapter Ten

PARTING THOUGHTS

So, we've gone through several narrative versions of vegetarianism - what to exclude, how often, what to call yourself in your new dietary role - then we raced through thousands of years of our ancestors' eating habits, arriving at what Germany and France are doing about the amount of meat they consume. As I'm half Italian, I thought I should also check the current eating habits of my mother's forefathers, and it appears that the Italian research institute Eurispes estimates that 10% of Italians are vegetarian and 1.1% are vegan. Wikipedia has an extensive list of countries, and the number of people therein who have stopped eating meat, but I was struck more by the speed and the numbers that are deciding to reduce or stop their meat consumption, in particular choosing to become vegan, which I feel is quite an extreme step to make by someone who regularly eats meat.

I also let you in to a secret about my rocky transition to vegetarianism, and my shameless theft of six lamb chops during the process. At the time, it was touch and go whether or not I would continue with the attempt because, in those days, you either ate meat and fish or you didn't. But Life is a compromise or you're stuffed, and after realising that I wanted to eat meat dishes but not animals, I was able to discover an alternative that worked for me. I hope you'll consider doing so yourself. From what you have read in this book, you'll know that the range of meat substitute foods available in the UK is extensive and, however you end up self-identifying (what a choice phrase that is!) I hope you found the information helpful (and accurate, Robert), and that it's given you the encouragement and the confidence to have a go at creating your own meat-free journey. You are a meat substitute/replacement virgin, and I envy you.

Printed in Great Britain
by Amazon